In the Eyes of Stone Dogs

In the Eyes of Stone Dogs

Daniel Danis

translated by

Linda Gaboriau

Talonbooks
Vancouver

Talonbooks
P.O. Box 2076, Vancouver, British Columbia, Canada V6B 3S3
www.talonbooks.com

Typeset in New Baskerville and printed and bound in Canada.

First Printing: 2005

Le Langue-à-langue des Chiens de Roche was first published in French in 2000 by Leméac Éditeur.

Library and Archives Canada Cataloguing in Publication
Danis, Daniel, 1962–
[Langue-à-langue des chiens de roche. English]
  In the eyes of stone dogs / Daniel Danis ; translated by Linda Gaboriau.

A play.
Translation of: Le langue-à-langue des chiens de roche.
ISBN 0-88922-519-2
  I. Gaboriau, Linda II. Title. III. Title: Langue-à-langue des chiens de roche. English.
PS8557.A5667L3613 2005   C842'.54   C2004-906436-3

The publisher gratefully acknowledges the financial support of the Canada Council for the Arts; the Government of Canada through the Book Publishing Industry Development Program; and the Province of British Columbia through the British Columbia Arts Council for our publishing activities.

In April, 1998, as part of the drama programme at the Conservatoire de Montréal, the first version of this play was presented in a series of performances directed by Claude Poissant.

In the fall of 1998, Théâtre Ouvert (Paris) sponsored the publication as a Tapuscrit, and a workshop followed by a staged reading directed by Michel Didym, of the second version entitled *La Langue des Chiens de Roche*.

The play premiered on January 10, 2001 at Théâtre d'Aujourd'hui (Montreal) in a production directed by René Richard Cyr, with the following cast and crew:

DJOUKIE:	Isabelle Roy
JOELLE:	Marie-France Lambert
GODDESS:	Dominique Quesnel
LEO SIMARD:	Pierre Collin
CHARLES:	Patrick Hivon
NIKI:	Sébastien Rajotte
SIMON:	Jean-François Pichette
MURIELLE:	Catherine Bonneau
COYOTE:	Normand D'Amour
Set design:	François Vincent
Costumes:	Marie-Pierre Fleury
Lighting:	Claude Accolas
Music:	Alain Dauphinais

In November 2001, the play premiered in France at Théâtre du Vieux-Colombier (Paris) in a production directed by Michel Didym.

The playwright received financial assistance from Fondation Beaumarchais (France), from Conseil des Arts et des Lettres du Québec and from the Canada Council for the Arts.

This translation was commissioned by the Tarragon Theatre, under the artistic direction of Urjo Kareda, and was first presented in a staged reading directed by Jackie Maxwell, produced by Tarragon Theatre (Toronto) in December 1999, in collaboration with Centre des auteurs dramatiques (CeAD).

PLACE

An imaginary island in the St. Lawrence River, subject to the cycle of the tides.

CHARACTERS

DJOUKIE, *15*
JOELLE, *31*
GODDESS, *31*
LEO SIMARD, *67*
CHARLES, *19*
NIKI, *15*
SIMON, *35*
MURIELLE, *17*
COYOTE, *age unknown*

The characters' hair should be distinctive.

DOGS
TWO DOGS *(male and female), watchdog-witnesses*
REX, *Joelle's dog*
246 DOGS, *in Leo's kennel*
OTHER ISLAND DOGS

The representation of the dogs on stage seems necessary and significant, but their number and the nature of their presence (visual or physical, through smell or sound) are to be determined. The two watchdog-witnesses are, however, present before the audience enters and when the audience leaves.

Are dogs the albino witnesses of our lives? They sleep more than they live awake, are we figments of their dreams? Are they the guardians of Aeschylus' wall?

Two DOGS observe the audience enter. The actors appear on stage, nine bodies spinning in the dark. The DOGS watch them. Blackout.

FIRST WAVE

Standing on a ladder outside the Gaz-O-Tee-Pee, DJOUKIE is holding a series of number 8s on wooden tiles.

DJOUKIE

Let it begin with a night wind, a warm, moist wind like at the beginning of humanity. From where I'm standing, I can see the houses, the streetlights on the other shore, and the last ferry docking at the red quay. I can make out the ploughed earth of what will become our neighbours' yellow corn field, and the grey road that snakes around the island. I can make out our mobile home parked beside our gas station, the Gaz-O-Tee-Pee. A real junkpile for a bunch of hopeless mental cases.

Joelle, it's archaic, making me climb a wobbly ladder to change the price of gas with numbers carved in wood.

JOELLE

Dammit, Djoukie, hurry up, I want to close.

DJOUKIE

I want a certainty now.

JOELLE

I busted my heart all day asking you to stop bugging me about a father you might have had.

DJOUKIE

The wind is blowing hard enough to strip the bark off trees! Let the breath of the wind blow into every orifice of my body, all the way to my secret cave, let it reveal my eggs and sow them with its misty drool, so love is born in me at last.

Earth wind, show me how to love, rather than bark.

JOELLE

Okay, Djoukie! Everyone knows you just won the Governor General's Medal for your brilliance at school. Stop foaming at the mouth and change the damn numbers.

DJOUKIE

This afternoon, at the awards ceremony, when I walked down the aisle of the auditorium, I saw all those gawking carp applauding like seals while I was muttering to myself: Is this the human race, this bunch of hopeless mental cases?

Besides, you could've congratulated me with a chocolate cake at least.

JOELLE

Shut up, Rex! Djoukie, I asked you if you wanted to invite some friends over. You told me you didn't have any. You don't know what you want anymore.

DJOUKIE

You hear that, the wind is carrying the howls from Simard's kennel. That's our hearts howling, we're all just the bastard pups of wailing bitches.

JOELLE

You can't help it, can you? The worse it gets, the more
you lay it on, the more you wallow in it.

DJOUKIE

There, now you've got your asshole 8s.

JOELLE

You think you're so smart, dumping the muck of your
highfalutin drama on everything in sight. You
shouldn't act so stuck-up, you won't escape the curse
of life. At your age, I'd already had you and nobody
came to rescue me from this bitch of a life. And it'll
be the same for you. You'll have to give life its due.

DJOUKIE

This woman whose head I'm clutching is my mother,
Joelle, and I speak these words to her: I'm going crazy,
I need an answer, a certainty, any certainty. Tell me
who the father I don't want to meet is, just give me the
guarantee I have one.

Why can't we go live on our ancestors' land, Ma?

Look at my feet on the ground, night is grabbing hold
of my feet, climbing up my body, suffocating me. The
layers of night weigh on my head like a cap of ten
thousand light years. Can you hear my heart buried in
so much gloom? My heart is howling, Ma.

I'm suffocating, suffocating, suffocating.

GODDESS

I've just walked out of the mobile home wearing my
goddaughter Djoukie's pretty medal round my neck,
Djoukie, who'd say in her saucy way that if I sink into
the gravel yard at the Gaz-O-Tee-Pee, I've only got my
big ass and my high heels to blame.

The woman I'm touching, Joelle, she's my friend, in my heart, my sister. We've been together since childhood. At seventeen, I married a guy nice as they come. This was his gas station. So I wouldn't feel lonely on the island, he invited Joelle and Djoukie to come live in a mobile home on the side of the lot.

A year after our wedding, my husband split an aneurysm. I ended up owner of the gas station. Joelle looks after the business. To attract the tourists, she got the idea of decorating the garage like a teepee, because of our roots. We even put up a sign that's round like our dreamcatchers.

Listen, the wind is whirling to the sound of a loud honking: that's Coyote.

My handsome wolf!

DJOUKIE
Great, look at Goddess, with the hair on her legs all abristle!

JOELLE
Behave yourself, Djoukie!

COYOTE
How's the girls-o-tee-pee?

JOELLE
I was about to close, Coyote.

GODDESS
Wow! You fresh-painted your jeep yellow!

COYOTE
I don't need gas, Joelle.

GODDESS
My handsome Coyote's so wild!

SIMON stands off to one side.

COYOTE

I've brought company!

COYOTE goes over to SIMON.

Don't be shy, Simon.

SIMON

(*speaking to COYOTE*) I wanted to come tomorrow, I would've worn something else.

COYOTE

Are you afraid I'll tell Joelle you stole that picture from me?

SIMON

Either hide it or give it back to me.

COYOTE

(*speaking to the others*) I won't be long!

(*to SIMON*) Pretty Joelle, all naked, her legs spread apart ...

He laughs.

SIMON

Don't be a troublemaker.

COYOTE

Joelle, I'd like you to meet my buddy, Simon. He's the ex-soldier I told you about, remember?

JOELLE

Sorry, my hands are dirty.

SIMON

Doesn't matter, ours must stink, we've just come from the slaughterhouse because of ... euhhhh.

COYOTE
The high wind of this evening blows between them, a scrap of chocolate bar wrapper flutters over their heads, their hair is ruffled.

I slip Joelle's picture into Simon's hand and, click!

DJOUKIE
Doesn't it make you sick, filling your fresh-painted yellow jalopy with animal remains?

COYOTE
It's my good deed, I'm delivering bones to Simard's kennel.

(*to SIMON*) I'm trying to butter up the old man who still thinks I was mixed up in his son Charles's arrest.

DJOUKIE
One helluva filthy junkpile.

JOELLE
Watch your vocabulary, Djoukie.

(*to SIMON*) They say you were in the army, that you were sent on a mission with the Blue Berets.

SIMON
Yeah, euhhhh …

JOELLE
Why are you looking at me like that?

COYOTE
Here, Rex, the biggest bone for the prettiest chops in town.

GODDESS
I want you to kidnap me tonight, you could make me bloom.

DJOUKIE
Great, now the sow wants her bone.

JOELLE
I chase my daughter and let her have it with a rag. I catch hold of her hair.

I speak these words to the one I'm holding by the hair: Last night, I was lying on my bed, thinking about you. I pictured myself talking to you. I can feel something coming, something serious, something horrible involving you.

If only I knew what to do to avoid this trouble for you. I feel paralysed, like I've been turned to stone by an imminent catastrophe. You who come from my belly, do you feel the same thing?

GODDESS
I love you both, my sweethearts, don't fight with each other.

COYOTE
I found a job for my buddy Simon. He starts tomorrow, replacing Colton, the town planner who died last month.

JOELLE
So, from now on, he's the one who'll come bug me.

SIMON
I don't get it.

JOELLE
Once you've stuck your nose in Colton's files, you'll see my name on the "contamination" list, because my neighbour, the farmer, has complained that his damn corn on the cob tastes of gas.

Yoohoo, stop eating me with your eyes!

SIMON

Euhhh ... I was daydreaming.

JOELLE

Listen, Coyote, don't you dare leave your ex-Blue
Beret in my yard while you take off with Goddess, I
don't feel like screwing tonight or any other night. Is
that clear, you meddler!

COYOTE

Don't get riled, Joelle, we were just stopping by.
Besides, you hear that, the dogs can tell I'm on my
way.

JOELLE

Good, ciao amigos! Goddess, don't show up in the
middle of the night, Djoukie has exams tomorrow.

GODDESS

Don't worry, sweetie, I'm going to play night owl till
the crack of dawn.

COYOTE

(*to SIMON*) I told you she was difficult. We'll try
another approach.

(*to GODDESS*) Climb aboard, my pretty goddess, we're
out of here.

GODDESS

Bye, my two sweeties.

SIMON

Ciao, euhhh, goodbye, I didn't want to eat you ...
euhhh. Bye!

JOELLE

Come, Rex, good boy!

DJOUKIE

The canary yellow jalopy sinks beneath the layers of night, with Goddess, in the back seat, a drunken land between two bags of bones.

And I disappear.

SECOND WAVE

In the Simards' yard, with the bags from the slaughterhouse.

NIKI

The edges of our house blend into the dark with only one door and two windows lit up to show where it stands.

CHARLES

Coyote just left, after unloading the grub for the dogs in our yard. If we only had a dozen of them, we might have enough for a week, but with two hundred and forty-six dogs—

LEO

Here, Niki, you take care of the grinder. Charles, don't tell me Coyote didn't slip something in your back pocket!

CHARLES

(*handing him the slip of paper*) Yes, Pa-Leo, a party this weekend on the shore.

LEO

(*holding the paper without looking at it*) Mother of Mars! Can't you recognize danger? If you go hanging out in crooked places, you'll end up in jail again, or worse, we'll be digging your grave.

CHARLES

Pa-Leo, don't fly off the handle, I won't go, don't worry.

LEO

You know Coyote's a troublemaking schemer. If we didn't have to feed these poor dogs, I'd kick him off our land. I'm sure he was mixed up in your ... you know what business.

NIKI takes the paper and reads it.

CHARLES

Pa-Leo, stop worrying ... about the dope, too, I swear, I don't take it anymore, I don't sell it anymore and I won't kill either.

LEO

I swore to your mother, Eva, that I'd make good and honest men of you and your brother. That guy who was with Coyote, I suppose he's some kinda crook too?

CHARLES

You're not gonna like it, but he's the new guy come to replace Colton.

LEO

Here we go, the greenhorns from the Society for the Defense of Animals will be back with their damn hygiene inspection business. They want to clear out our kennel. I don't want you to leave me alone, boys, not for one second. We'll be waiting for them with my gun, just like two months ago. The new guy will show up, that's for sure.

Keep grinding, I'll take a ration to the dogs.

CHARLES

The one I grab by the head and hold to my forehead
is my brother, Niki, a happy-go-lucky idiot I love.

Niki, I feel like I've turned into a total worrier. Smell
my underarm. Do I smell of worry?

NIKI

I won't smell you if you don't take me to Coyote's
party. I want to go to the rage on the shore, my heart's
all lovesick.

CHARLES

We'll see, smell first!

NIKI

It smells really strong. Poor Charles!

CHARLES

Even the dogs, when they smell me, they start barking
to warn me of danger. I'm running on nightmares. Do
you ever dream about our mother?

NIKI

Yes, and it's always merry. My dreams are tangled in
red, blue and yellow.

CHARLES

And mine in black. She always sends me back to the
void. Coyote says my mother was a good woman and it
must be my conscience that comes disguised as
Ma-Eva's ghost.

NIKI

To the brother I press to my chest, I speak these
words: Go on making your sculptures, even if Pa-Leo
thinks it's useless. Go on bruising your hands with the
flat rocks and the drifting branches you use to build
your arches. Go on building them on the shore even if

the tides come to swallow them. I think those are the only times you look less tortured.

Charles, I want to build happiness with a girl who might be going to the rage party.

CHARLES
> I won't take you there. You're too young. It can get dangerous. After their dances, it always turns into an orgy.

NIKI
> It's Djoukie Newhouse.

CHARLES
> How can you be interested in a brainy girl like her?

NIKI
> Take me along, just for a while.

CHARLES
> No is no. Anyway, there's already been two of those parties and I never saw her there.

NIKI
> You and your damn worry-smelling, next time, you can keep it to your criminal self!

And I'm gone.

THIRD WAVE

Outside the Gaz-O-Tee-Pee.

DJOUKIE
> Day breaks like all the others, with the usual degree of horror. Murielle, the neurotic who thinks she's a top model, arrives at the Gaz-O-Tee-Pee.

It's alright, Joelle, finish your omelet, I'll go.

Hi! Can I fill up your petal-bike?

MURIELLE
Ha, ha! Don't be so wise, Djoukie. I just want to buy some water from the vending machine.

DJOUKIE
You've come all this way, decked out like that, to buy a bottle of water.

MURIELLE
I just wanted ... Have you finished your exams?

DJOUKIE
No, I've got three left.

MURIELLE
Alright, I dive right in and come out with it. For Summer Solstice, Coyote's organizing another one of those rage parties down on the shore, and since I don't have any girlfriends, can you tell me what you think, if I went looking like this?

DJOUKIE
Before going to the rage, you better find yourself a boyfriend, because I bet, even at your age, you've never shown your big slit to anyone.

MURIELLE
Stop, don't rub it in, I'm embarrassed already. I thought, 'cause once I asked you to be in the school play with me, that you'd—

DJOUKIE
Okay, forget the small talk. Walk around a bit. Forgive me, in advance, if I say what I think.

MURIELLE

If I show up looking like this ...

DJOUKIE

You'll look like a crab. You want to look sensuous. You're not going to a shopping mall. Sensuous!

MURIELLE

Like this? I don't look like a frog? I brought some accessories.

DJOUKIE

Hurry up, before a customer comes.

MURIELLE

Some little leopard cigars and a flask of vodka and orange. What do you think, if I arrive at the party walking like this. Sssss!

DJOUKIE

No, stop, you look ridiculous.

MURIELLE

Tell me at least if you think I'm too fat? What about my breasts, are they too small or too pointy?

Do you want to come to the party with me?

DJOUKIE

Listen to me, you dummy, I'm not your sister. You'll never be my friend because you're too superficial.

MURIELLE

You can't see my distress. I want to go to the rage to experience love, for a first and last time, because, tomorrow, I will no longer exist ... the final journey!

DJOUKIE

Everybody knows you try to make friends by playing the future suicide victim. Don't bore me with your

crap about the final journey. Just do it once and for
all, you crab.

MURIELLE
It's true that you're just an uncivilised bitch.

JOELLE
I'll replace you now, Djoukie. Go study instead.

DJOUKIE
(*to MURIELLE*) Have a good final journey, woof, woof!

MURIELLE
(*to DJOUKIE*) Ssssss!

> *DJOUKIE exits.*

And I take off.

> *SIMON enters carrying a box of chocolates and a
> briefcase.*

JOELLE
You still walk like a soldier; there's going to be trouble.

SIMON
(*eating chocolates*) You could say hello, Joelle.

Hi, Rex!

JOELLE
Down, Rex.

When you come as a friend, I'll say hello, but I can
see, you've got my file in your hands, on a Saturday
morning. Bravery beyond the call of duty! Just like in
the army.

SIMON
I've come as a friend.

JOELLE

As he goes to step onto our boardwalk, he trips and
the box of chocolates wrapped in metallic paper goes
flying into the air: nice mess!

SIMON

Euhhh ... would you love-like ... a chocolate? To
impress my first girlfriend, I convinced her that I had
killed a dog with my own two hands.

JOELLE

Well, I killed a crocodile with my knife.

SIMON

(*eating a chocolate*) A real crocodile ... around here?

JOELLE

Okay, get to the point, what do you want?

SIMON

The samples taken from the subsoil don't meet the
standards. I even ate one of your neighbour's frozen
ears of corn. It really does taste of diesel.

JOELLE

And I'm supposed to pay for the decontamination out
of my own pocket! No way! The bank warned me, one
more financial setback and they'll make me declare
bankruptcy.

Lots of people would love to see us close down.
Especially those schemers at Town Hall who'd be
happy to see us take off so they can build the road to
the future harbour. The road out front could pass
right through here. They wouldn't have to pay for any
other expropriations. And it would make three less
Indian women on their territory!

SIMON is still eating his chocolates.

SIMON
(*staggering*) I'm losing my bearings, I can feel it.

When I was abroad on that mission, I blew my top, for
a second I was like a gorilla on the rampage. When I
talk about it, people look at me like I'm from outer
space. Anyway, as long as wars don't take place on
home territory, they're all imaginary.

Then, I fall to the ground from hypoglycemia.

JOELLE
I get a cold towel. To revive him. He says to me: Too
little sugar in my blood, it's the second time it's
happened ...

SIMON
... at least, something overwhelming is finally
happening in my life.

JOELLE
Don't kid yourself, soldier, I've got a busted heart.

SIMON
To the woman I hold like this, I speak these words: My
heart's got a hard-on for you. I dream of you. Skin to
skin. Making a baby together. Making life.

And I beat a hasty retreat.

FOURTH WAVE

In Coyote's yard, NIKI is battered and bloodstained.

NIKI
The voice we hear in the distance is mine. I get beat
up by three guys, the same three guys who were
friends with the one my brother killed, two years ago.

I'm not scared. Nothing serious can happen to me, I've already been visited by death.

Every time those guys run into me in the mist or some dark corner, they beat me up. My brother's on probation, if he gets into trouble, he can end up in jail again. That's why I never tell him when I get pushed around. It's my way of protecting him, I do it out of love.

A girl has lit firecrackers in my heart. Pa-Leo says if my smile gets any broader, my ears are gonna come unglued.

COYOTE and GODDESS are screwing in the jeep.

COYOTE
I think I heard someone in the yard.

GODDESS
Over here, in the jeep!

What happened to you, sweet Niki?

NIKI
I fell off my bike on my way over here.

Coyote, I want to go to the rage party, but Charles won't let me. He's afraid I'll drink some of your love liquor.

COYOTE
My purple love punch!

GODDESS
Same thing happens every time, I'm always losing my boob brace.

She searches for her bra.

COYOTE

  You got your heart hooked on Joelle's girl?

NIKI

  Oh, who told you that? Charles?

GODDESS

  On Djoukie!? Come over here, let me give you a kiss,
  Niki!

  She kisses him.

NIKI

  Ouch!

GODDESS

  Sorry, pup, but I'm too glad! Wow, you're really
  banged up!

COYOTE

  I go inside and come out with a bottle of love liquor.

  The minute Djoukie takes a sip, she'll want to make
  love with you right on the spot.

NIKI

  What? It's not made so she'll fall in love with me?

COYOTE

  In a way, yeah, let's just say it's made to whet desire.

NIKI

  The desire to love?

GODDESS

  I think he's missing the point.

COYOTE

  Right!

GODDESS

  Do you know how to French kiss?

NIKI

What do you mean, French?

COYOTE

We mean, French kiss Djoukie or some girl, for heaven's sake!

NIKI

French kiss, I think about this word. It must have something to do with touching her sweater breasts or her dressed-up bum.

COYOTE

A real tongue-to-tongue, tongue-to-tongue!?

COYOTE starts laughing extravagantly.

NIKI

(*nervously*) I don't know what that means, but I know death, it's already visited me.

COYOTE

Whoa! Relax. Watch this.

GODDESS

We press our mouths together and our tongues slither around in our saliva. They devour each other.

He sticks out his tongue. GODDESS does, too. They touch the tip of each other's tongue.

NIKI

Ooohhh! Tongue-to-tongue is beautiful!

COYOTE

Hey, Niki! Come over here! Do you know how a girl is made?

NIKI

What do you mean, made?

COYOTE

Goddess, the backseat madonna, will show you her pretty pond.

GODDESS lies down, COYOTE pulls up her skirt.

NIKI

Ooohhh! It's beautiful!

GODDESS

(*laughing*) You're beautiful.

COYOTE

Niki, that pond is where you plant your bullrush.

NIKI

Nature is a beautiful thing! Does everyone go bullrushing?

COYOTE

Yes, you silly boy. Look at this, it's a bud you put to your mouth to make a girl bloom.

When you think all lives come out of this pond! Mercy!

Loud laughter.

GODDESS

He left, beaming his head off, saying: I won't need your purple love liquor.

NIKI

That's not what I want with Djoukie, I'm thirsty for love, I mean, for something unique and marvellous.

COYOTE

Beneath these blue skies, blessed are the innocent, they shall inherit the earth, for they possess secret happiness.

FIFTH WAVE

In the Simards' yard.

LEO

(*with a rifle slung over his shoulder*) I'm on the roof with my son, fixing the antenna.

Mother of Mars, Charles! I just saw Niki coming out of Coyote's yard.

I grab your ear, don't move, I might pull it off and you wouldn't hear what I'm gonna tell you and you're gonna repeat to your fool of a brother: Coyote is an animal. He was born from a hole in the ground, no father, no mother, he was dressed like a furry animal and one day, he discovered he could shed his fur coat whenever he wanted.

CHARLES

C'mon, Pa-Leo, you're more than a little paranoid. When night falls, he's always cold, even in the middle of the summer, that's why he wears a fur coat and is nicknamed Coyote.

LEO

A clown who thinks he's a god! He invented the worst of all monkeyshine miseries: sickness, death, winter!

A troublemaker of the worst kind: even the mosquitoes are his making!

CHARLES

Stop, Pa-Leo! At least I was free of you in jail.

LEO mutters inaudible words, snivelling.

Don't pretend to cry. What did you say? Yes, yes, you'll always be my loving father, you don't have to worry about me.

LEO

Then you can do what you want, and think what you want of him.

SIMON enters, CHARLES slips away.

SIMON

Mr. Simard!

LEO

Look at that, come to pester me in my own yard. Charles!?

Can't trust them for a minute, good thing I asked them to stick close to me.

SIMON

Hello, I'm Coyote's friend and I—

LEO

Drop the introductions, I know who you are.

SIMON

I came to meet you, have a little talk. Could you come down here? People have filed dozens of complaints about your kennel.

LEO

Lots of idle badmouthing!

SIMON

Is it true that the dogs live year-round in the house?

LEO

There's dog everywhere: in the upstairs bedrooms, in the bathroom, in the kitchen, on the broken-down furniture in the living room, in the cupboards and

31

closets, on the floor, on the veranda, outside under the porch, in the old car without an engine and sometimes in their kennels.

LEO puts down his rifle.

I'm not gonna harm you. Unstiffen a bit, you're not wearing a uniform anymore.

SIMON

Mr. Simard, before getting the police involved in these complaints, I'd like us to attempt—

LEO

You look pretty nervous. Maybe you've been reading too much of their bitching? Instead of embarking on a war, you bundle of nerves, take a little puppy. Open your heart to him, talk to him. Makes you feel safe when you get rushes of fear. I got forty-two bitches who sleep in my room, it's for their protection because the big males could eat their litters.

Don't you think I look calm?

Ha, ha, ha! He left, with a puppy in his arms, under the afternoon skies.

SIXTH WAVE

On the shore.

CHARLES

The sun is about to set on the west shore. It's blinding me practically. I can hear the tide rising. I'm waiting to see my rock-and-branch uselessness disappear.

Who's there? Who's there? Here I go, nightmaring wide awake. The voice that speaks these words to me is

the voice of Ma-Eva: Can you see me sitting on the
long smooth rock worn by time, where I've set up my
jars, the ones I used for my preserves? I'm unrolling
inner tubes, can you see me? I'm filling them with
your old clothes. You see what I'm doing, I'm stuffing
you back into tubes. Look at me, brat! I'm spreading
my legs, I push the inner tube stuffed like a sausage
into my vagina and I say: This is what you deserve, you
deserve to return to the nothing of nothingness.

The sun dies and my work of the day is swept away in a
coffin of water.

And I slip off.

SEVENTH WAVE

*In Coyote's yard as he finishes filling cases with his
bottles of aphrodisiac drinks.*

GODDESS
Simon, come help us cap the bottles for the rage.

SIMON
I'm in no mood for partying. It's like there's a little
Simon going 'round in circles in my head. Making me
dizzy. I don't know what's wrong with me.

COYOTE
Well, with what you went through on your mission,
and the army kicking you out for behaviour problems,
and then your wife replacing you with a high-ranking
officer, I guess that's enough to make a man feel lousy.
Get ready: the worst is yet to come—you don't know
what it's like to mull things over on an island.

On an island, you feel separate and united at the same time. Your body is united by the ground, but it's also separate from the rest of the world, even if the other shore is only an hour by ferry.

Everyone who leaves, and they all leave sooner or later, ends up missing the island. Most of them come back, but nothing is any better. A deep uneasiness has settled in their bodies because they discovered they're not at peace anywhere, not on the island or anywhere else. Sometimes violence is all they have to express their discomfort. Sometimes the violence is so overwhelming, they could pound someone to death. That's one of the reasons I invented my rage parties for release. People here on this island buy dogs to beat them and abandon them after.

By the way, you never gave me Joelle's picture back. It's the only one where she's all naked. Back in those days, she was pretty wild.

GODDESS
Don't waste your time hanging 'round here, Simon. Joelle won't come to the rage party. She put her senses to sleep years ago and she refuses to let anyone wake her up.

GODDESS chuckles. CHARLES and NIKI enter from a distance.

NIKI
Let me come.

CHARLES
Djoukie won't be there. Go back home. I don't go to the party, I play watchguard, in case the pigs come showing their snouts.

NIKI

Criminal!

CHARLES

If I see Djoukie walk by, I'll come get you, I swear.

NIKI

Promise?

CHARLES

Come, let me give you a hug.

> *NIKI turns away, disappointed. CHARLES enters Coyote's house.*

Hello, Simon!

SIMON

Right ... hello!

CHARLES

I hear Pa-Leo gave you a beautiful puppy! Don't worry about my father, he's as harmless as his blank-bullet rifle.

COYOTE

Hey, the artist! Load the cases into my jeep.

SIMON

Here, Coyote, here's the picture.

COYOTE

I race over to my padlocked chest and take out two bottles of very special liquor, very "Coyote," very red, very different from the black, yellow and purple punches for the rage.

Here, Simon, for you, along with the picture. Drink it thinking about her.

SIMON

What goes on at your rage party, are you all going to sing: We want paradise now?

COYOTE starts laughing extravagantly.

COYOTE

Just starry skies. Rages are rituals to release your heart through your mouth, your brain through your ass, your tongue through your belly and your sex through the palm of your hands.

GODDESS

If you come to one of Coyote's parties, flip the switch on your brain and let the rest of your body take over your life. If you want, handsome Simon, I could initiate you.

COYOTE

That, buddy, is paradise lost in person.

Goddess, give him a Frenchie.

SIMON

No, thank you all the same.

COYOTE

When we get there, we find some dry wood, we light a fire, we smoke, we drink, we dance on the shore. I will have driven my old jeep up close, with the speakers on the hood, and we let the music roll till midnight.

At midnight, on the dot, I pass out my aphrodisiac drinks. Romeo and his Turbos will rev up the tam-tams and everybody will chant:

We want starry skies, we want sweet sex.

An hour later, everyone's taken their clothes off, and all the mindless bodies start rubbing against each other and end in an orgy.

GODDESS tries to caress SIMON playfully.

SIMON
Goddess, please stop.

CHARLES
Here we go, Coyote, people are arriving.

In the distance, voices are chanting:

VOICES
We want starry skies, we want sweet sex.

GODDESS
Yahoo, I'm wet already!

COYOTE
Charles, get the lantern. If you see trouble headed our way, come warn me.

Tonight, there'll be quite a climax when the Tom-Dick-and-Harries decide to screw a she-dog.

Climb aboard, Simon.

SIMON
No, I think I'll try your beverage at home by my lonesome.

EIGHTH WAVE

Suspended time.

NIKI
Niki is calling Djoukie.

Djoukie appears.

The one I'm holding by the hand, I'm going to meet her soon. I'm thinking about you so hard I can see you, I speak these words to you: One day, in town, I saw a man bare-naked on the only avenue on the island, in the middle of winter, naked, not even shoes on his feet. He was shouting: Love to the rescue! He was bald, with a big belly, skinny little legs, so bad you could see his bones.

The snow was melting, but it was cold. I was sitting in the bus. Waving his arms in the air, the old man was shouting: Love to the rescue! Love to the rescue!

People were laughing, honking their horns. My eyes were gaping with fear when he walked by my window with his blue lips and his voice all ragged from shouting: Love to the rescue! Love to the rescue!

He slipped on a big strip of ice, and fell flat on his back, banging his head on the sidewalk, foaming at the mouth, he kept on yelling: Love to the rescue! Love to the rescue!

Let's disappear now.

End of suspended time.

NINTH WAVE

At Charles's lookout post.

MURIELLE
Unsmokable, these little leopard cigars. I walk along the road to the shore. If I keep going, I'll get to the party. I'm too embarrassed.

But suddenly, on top of Walrus Head Rock, I can make out a beautiful silhouette.

I walk over to the man who's going to make a woman of me tonight. To become a woman for the first time and the last ... maybe, we'll see.

I creep alongside a hedge of uneatable berries. My tongue is full of Sssss ... Ssss ...

CHARLES
Who goes there? Oh, no, I'm imagining things again. Is anyone there?

MURIELLE
Ssssssssss ...

CHARLES
I can't see you. If you've come for the rage party, go ahead fast, otherwise, go blow dry your teeth somewhere else.

MURIELLE
Sssss! I'm dancing like a cobra, can't you see what I want. I'm all decked out to whet your appetite, I want to become a woman, a real woman. Sssss ... Ssssss ... You don't know how much it means to me. Take me, behind this hedge of uneatable red berries.

CHARLES
Don't come too close, I'm on guard. If you want to get laid, go down to the shore.

MURIELLE
Sssss ... Sssss ...

He leaps down off the rock and heads toward me, I act more enticing. He takes me. I don't resist. I'm panting, I want to impress him, I look all wide-eyed like in the videos my parents rent on weekends and that I watch on Sunday mornings.

I like the smell of dog you wear on your jacket.

CHARLES

I get down on my knees in front of you, I take off your panties. Behind the hedge of uneatable berries, I lift you up and push you against Walrus Head Rock, I hold you there with my chest, my tongue is in your mouth, your eyes are wide open when I take out my dick. Your hole isn't wet enough.

Spit in my hand.

MURIELLE

I want it, but I'm afraid of him all the same. It happens so fast. I should have asked him to sleep with me. Maybe that's what taking meant for him. But I meant lying in the moss near the hedge of uneatable berries, in each other's arms, in a more, much more …

CHARLES

I smooth your saliva on my sex and enter you without warning.

MURIELLE

I thought it would feel good, that it would turn me on like the girls in the videos.

I zap you, I rewind you, I never saw you.

CHARLES

What did you expect? Nothing more to be said. As boring as that.

MURIELLE

Do you do it standing up with all your women?

CHARLES
Look at me, did you really expect paradise?

MURIELLE
I recognize you, your name is Charles. You're the criminal!

CHARLES
I grab your head: I'm not a criminal even if I did spend two years in the jail for minors. It was his own fault, the pusher fell into the water. We'd exchanged the dope and the money, he wanted to take it back with a gun. He'd already shown me his plastic gun, guess he didn't remember. I told him to get lost. He jumped me, we both fell into the water, he didn't know how to swim. He drowned. I couldn't save him. They accused me of being an unpremeditated criminal, but I know I'm not one.

Here, here's your hole-hider with the little hearts on it.

Beat.

MURIELLE
I didn't want it like that. Not that rough way. I'm not quite a woman, and at the same time I'm no longer a little girl.

At least take me for a drink, some refreshments.

CHARLES
Impossible, I'm on guard. I've got a thermos full of coffee, you want some?

MURIELLE
I feel like telling him: Soon, maybe, I'm going to die, I feel so all alone in this world.

I've seen you riding on an old motorcycle. You've hidden it.

CHARLES

I didn't bring it, I snuck out.

We have a long talk and she asks me to start over again, but this time, she undresses me and kisses me, we lie down naked on the moss behind the hedge of uneatable berries.

TENTH WAVE

Farther off, on the shore, the ragers' voices chant:

VOICES

We want starry skies, we want sweet sex.

GODDESS

Coyote, why don't you want us to live together all the time?

COYOTE

(*carrying a case of bottles*) You're a pain when you're drunk!

Listen, Goddess, things are great the way they are. We each have our own place, we do what we want. Let go of me, can't you see I'm in a hurry. Come help me serve the drinks instead.

GODDESS

(*alone*) I am inhabited by a lost land that calls to me. I drown it for a few hours here on the shore, because the beauty of the trees hurts, the sunsets tug at my heart, the rivers swollen with mercury wrench my guts, the clouds heavy with acid make me cry, and the smell of the contaminated wind is killing me.

And I flee.

ELEVENTH WAVE

Outside the Gaz-O-Tee-Pee.

DJOUKIE

Joelle, you hear that barking in the night. You think it's the dogs? You're wrong.

It always happens under the cover of night, once the layers of night have bedded down, one on top of the other ... Look, after sunset, night begins on the ground, another night arrives on top of that and dark finally fills the sky. Then dawn comes and throws off the covers.

It's right in the middle of the night, when the layers of darkness crush the roofs of the sleeping islanders, when the souls of dreamy people are bogged down and can't wander like they want. That's when they start to howl. What you hear is the dreamy souls barking 'cause they're pinned to this damn rocky earth.

Ma, tell me what I can do to ease my heart.

JOELLE

To be loved, first you'd have to be loveable, you'd have to take off your angry armour.

DJOUKIE

If only you loved me, it would help me believe that love exists!

JOELLE

Even if someone came to declare his love to you, your dark heart would start to bark.

DJOUKIE

How do we love? With what, Ma?

JOELLE

With whatever you can.

DJOUKIE

You should have given me a father, or a man who might have been your lover. That would have made a false-father for me to love and given my little girl's heart some practice. But that would've meant getting involved, so instead you—

JOELLE

(*almost barking*) Shut up! Shut up!

TWELFTH WAVE

On the path, in the distance, voices still can be heard chanting:

VOICES

We want starry skies, we want sweet sex.

NIKI

The dense darkness prevents us from hurrying along the path that leads to our house.

CHARLES

Pa-Leo, give me my clothes back. It's embarrassing. Give me my shoes at least!

LEO

What kind of hounddog, bare-naked game were you playing, you twisted muzzlehead?!

CHARLES

I was standing guard, Pa-Leo.

LEO

Help me, Eva, my patience is sinking into a swamp of discouragement. A naked watchguard screwing around behind a hedge. I've seen it all!

CHARLES

Niki, if I grab hold of your hair, I'll twist your brains out!

NIKI

I wouldn't have told, if you'd taken me with you.

LEO

Niki, if I ever catch you going to that bare-nakedness on the shore, watch out! And you, dopey, you know those masquerade parties are forbidden! You want to end up in jail again, Mother of Mars!

NIKI

(*to CHARLES*) Maybe I could have met my future wife.

CHARLES

Pa-Leo, I've cut the sole of my foot.

LEO

Stick your tongue on it and walk!

CHARLES

Pa-Leo!

LEO

Eva!

NIKI

The SDA is right, when the wind is high, you can hear
our dogs at dusk.

LEO hands Charles's clothes to NIKI.

LEO

Here, Niki, take Charles's clothes and go see to the
dogs, but don't let them out of the kennel. We don't
want them to bark even more, got enough trouble as
is.

CHARLES

Pa-Leo, my foot is going to be the death of me.

LEO

He breaks my heart with his new man's voice, the
voice he will have for the rest of his life.

Here I come, my moonstruck mongrel.

NIKI

Charles, tell me if you saw her?

CHARLES

No, Niki, your Djoukie Newhouse wasn't there.

NIKI

Don't shout her name to the ends of the earth, you
wind-up moron!

CHARLES

I see my brother Niki tramp through a wall of barking
to get to our house. I can't get mad at this happy idiot,
in love with a girl he doesn't even know.

LEO

Stand up, don't make your old man bend over for
nothing.

CHARLES

It's really bleeding.

LEO

Mother of Mars! Climb on my back.

CHARLES

I'm too heavy, Pa-Leo.

LEO

You underestimate my strength, boy.

CHARLES

The man carrying me naked on his back with his
scratchy wool jacket, I love him. He does his best with
fathering.

Beat.

LEO

Feel any better?

CHARLES

Yes, thanks, Pa-Leo. You're a lot stronger than I
thought.

We walk for a while, in silence.

LEO

Mercy, it's far. I thought we were closer.

CHARLES

It's because of the wind bearing down all of a sudden,
and the night fog rising.

LEO

Don't try to avoid the subject, tomorrow we have to
talk about your bare-nakedness.

CHARLES

And the navy blue fog enveloped us for the rest of the way.

THIRTEENTH WAVE

In Simon's apartment.

SIMON

While I unchange my clothes for the third time today, my puppy lies sound asleep on the floor, on top of my dirty clothes.

SIMON takes a long sip of red liquor.

How do I walk, how do I think? If I walk like a soldier, do I think like one? If I walk like an astronaut, am I any lighter? And like this?

Beat.

SIMON finishes the rest of the bottle.

It feels like I'm split in two. I'm here and there at the same time. That guy over there is crawling on the ground, moving through the thick fog all the way to the corn field next to Joelle's house. And there she is, standing in her bedroom window.

SIMON is calling JOELLE.

JOELLE appears. Enigmatic, she listens, her eyes wide open. Their heads seem to be two planets in the universe.

To the woman whose hand I'm holding, I speak these words: My damn images of war keep filling my head. I was with my regiment. We were doing surveillance in a chain of hills. I remember, I was making the rounds

48

with a detachment when we witnessed, without budging, the massacre of two Gypsy families. You hear me, Joelle?

We're standing guard on top of a hill. We watch some armed men break down the door and barge into a house out in the country. Even though we're a ways off, the echo in the hills relays the panic. Gunshots. Silence, screams, silence, screams. We listen. Even the birds have stopped singing. We wait. Those are our orders, we have to wait. Half an hour later, the armed men come out.

After they leave, we go to the scene in our armoured cars. The parents are riddled with bullets, chopped up into pieces. The two kids are crucified on the wooden walls with nails in their shoulders and another in the mouth. I unnailed the youngest one. I carried him in my arms to our campsite. The smell of blood in the heat made me dizzy. I was going crazy, you have no idea, Joelle, the horrors you can accumulate in a war, and that one was one too many.

I thought while I was carrying him that he opened his eyes and smiled at me. I shouldn't have, I shouldn't have laid the kid down on his back on the ground ... or taken out my knife to slit open his belly, or thrown earth into his belly, shouting: "Come back to life, come back to life, come back to life."

Twenty-four hours later, I was back in this country. I underwent the psychological, medical tests. Three weeks later, in the big court martial hearing room, in front of the high-ranking officers, they discharged me.

For a year and a half now I've been asking myself how you make life. I want to create life, life, life.

JOELLE disappears. REX starts barking. JOELLE enters.
SIMON is lying on the ground.

JOELLE

In the morning, he was lying there under my window, curled up like a dog: What are you doing here? What do you want from me?

FOURTEENTH WAVE

On the shore, in the morning. COYOTE starts laughing extravagantly.

COYOTE

What a dump, the shore after a rage!

Don't forget to clean up in the love bushes.

CHARLES

Coyote, what should we do with the bitch?

COYOTE

Burn her with the rest of the garbage. A she-dog full of sperm from the Tom-Dick-and-Harries, stoned by thousands of rocks thrown in rage.

FIFTEENTH WAVE

Outside the Gaz-O-Tee-Pee.

DJOUKIE

All day, the wind blew up our nostrils and spun our reason into a whirl. When there's too much wind in your head, you always give birth to a storm.

I look at Goddess who looks like a silly jerk with her 3-D glasses that still smell of the cereal box.

JOELLE
O.K. Don't make one of your scenes tonight.

You've packed your bags? You going camping?

DJOUKIE
That depends on your answers.

GODDESS
What have you whipped up for us tonight, sweetie?
I'm hungry.

DJOUKIE
Tonight I haven't whipped up anything, make do with what's on the table.

(to JOELLE) How come you never talk to me?

JOELLE
What do you mean, never! You think I'm a non-stop television set? Wait, Goddess, we'll open some canned meat.

DJOUKIE
Where did the two of you hang out all day?

JOELLE
We went for a drive and a talk. We stopped to have a drink.

GODDESS
To talk about personal stuff.

DJOUKIE
Personal, my ass, the backseat madonna! Every time you think you're pregnant, I wake up in the middle of the night and I can feel your big anxiety-ass lying in

my busted spring bed. In the morning, I notice my breast is wet with your drool, Goddess!

GODDESS

You're wrong, when I crawl into your bed, it's because I had a nightmare about rapists and I'm crying.

DJOUKIE

No, it's because you know that soon you'll be spreading your legs at the abortion clinic on the other shore, so they can suction the bottom of your barrel. Go find your Coyote, you beer-sodden bitch.

GODDESS

I don't understand you anymore, Djoukie, you used to help me want to live, you had a giving heart.

JOELLE

Did you manage to study today?

DJOUKIE

Since when do you worry about me?

JOELLE

Alright, I know what's on your mind. The certainty that I'm your mother, isn't that enough?

DJOUKIE

Since when have you been a mother? In our house, I'm the one who's been Goddess's mother for years now. Isn't that true? We had to clean her up, sober her up, take care of her. And I had to cook for both of you, because the stove is in the mobile home, while Madam was happily working behind her counter or resting in her own little room.

GODDESS

You see that slice of bread and peanut butter? I drew your face with raspberry jam and what am I going to say?

DJOUKIE

We know—fat Goddess is about to eat little Djoukie. Stupid cow!

JOELLE

When you were little, you used to make us laugh with your playacting. But for the past four years, you've been playing the same character with the same sullen moods.

GODDESS

(*preparing another slice of bread*) Well, I should play in a porn movie. I'm just a big pile of flesh, and like a garden, I'm good for nothing till men buckle down and plough me.

Lewd laugh from GODDESS.

DJOUKIE

Joelle, come talk to me.

JOELLE

Even if you sweeten your temper for me, I'll never tell you who your father is. Shut up, Rex!

DJOUKIE

Joelle, why are we unhappy bastard women? Mama?!

GODDESS

(*still laughing*) Welcome to the adult world, our little medal-winner!

REX barks.

DJOUKIE

I grab the woman by the hair, I throw her on the ground and kick her silly.

Goddam black cow, filthy, stinking bitch.

JOELLE

Djoukie! You're going to hurt her. Stop! You're losing your mind!

DJOUKIE

The mindless one goes over to the forest-green toolbox and takes out the blowtorch. She unscrews the cap on the gas tank and she lights the torch.

JOELLE

Here we go, the grand finale in your highfalutin drama.

DJOUKIE

Tell me, tell me who my father is, or I'll toss this into the tank.

JOELLE

Get away from that tank, then we'll talk.

DJOUKIE

Tell us what I saw last winter when I came to knock on your window on the side of the garage. You remember, I was crying because Goddess was throwing up her guts, go ahead, tell us.

Why didn't you ever want me to come sleep with you in your room, in your bed? Why didn't you ever want to come back into the mobile home?

JOELLE

Shut up, Rex. You know why, twice they've come to steal the money I keep on the side. If you want to continue your studies, it's better for me to sleep in the store to protect our earnings.

DJOUKIE

You've been sleeping there for eight years and you leave me in that stupid junkpile of a stinking mobile home.

JOELLE

Rex, shut your trap, damn dog!

Djoukie, I thought about making my room bigger, but pretty soon you'll be moving away for your studies.

DJOUKIE

Tell us, tell us why you never wanted your dear daughter in your bed.

JOELLE

Dammit, Djoukie, turn off that flame.

DJOUKIE

Your dog gets to sleep with you.

JOELLE

Blow everything up! I don't give a damn!

DJOUKIE

Tell us, you're a dog-loving woman!

JOELLE

YES! YES! Four-legged dogs are no worse than two-legged ones. So there, are you happy?

DJOUKIE

So I'm the child of a dog, a dog!

JOELLE

Don't start in with your sick stories!

DJOUKIE

I just figured out why you don't love me. I'm the fruit of the mating between a woman and a dog. I am the living proof of your hazy actions.

JOELLE

I take the blowtorch out of her hands.

I don't know what prevents me from punching you in your melodramatic face. You have no idea what life stole from me. My heart is empty, I love you with my head, accept it, that's how it is.

GODDESS

Sweethearts, my two sweethearts, your tongues are adrift, bound for disaster. Let's stick together, the three of us.

DJOUKIE

Life is a miserable mistake! One miserable mistake!

JOELLE

Djoukie, come back. We'll sleep together tonight.

DJOUKIE

(*running off with her backpack*) Life is one miserable mistake.

JOELLE

Djoukie!

GODDESS

The wind blows between us and raises a fistful of dust that glows yellow from the streetlights. The fog rose suddenly, taking our sweetheart under its wing, our little Djoukie.

Seagull feathers and tears swirl in the air.

SIXTEENTH WAVE

In the Simards' yard.

LEO

I'm lucky I've still got the strength to put in a hard day's work!

Every morning when I wake up, I sit on the side of my bed for a good five minutes. I look out the window. And I say to myself, I just spent another night in good health. I got a few aches and pains, but at my age, I can't complain, I don't walk with a cane, I don't have to take pills to sleep at night or to live through the day. Day after day, I thank the Good Lord for granting me my health so I can go on caring for my boys.

My sons, they're still so young, my handsome boys!

MURIELLE

Evening, Mr. Simard. I'm the girl—

LEO

I grab your noggin like this so you get it into your thick skull that my son Charles needs a nice girl with lots of common sense, not some fornication contraption who hides behind hedges of vice. Don't play with my son's emotionality.

MURIELLE

Old limp balls!

I'm fed up, fed up with every inch of my skin, fed up with being horrendously nice. I can even shit niceness. Makes me sick to my stomach.

I'm sick to death of living like this! Sick to death of living, period!

LEO

Aie ya aie!

CHARLES

You've met each other?

LEO

(*to CHARLES*) I'm not sure she's too stable.

CHARLES

Pa-Leo, keep your comments to yourself.

LEO

You louse of a kid! Get over here, so I can talk you in the face.

You've got me worried. Niki's no better, he used to stick around the house, now he's running around. Have you seen the blue blows on his body?

CHARLES

You know how he is, always got his head in the clouds. No wonder he falls off his bike.

LEO

Exactly, Mother of Mars! Go get Niki, before he knocks himself silly. And get back here fast, both of you. The SDA is on their way, I can feel it.

CHARLES

C'mon, Pa-Leo, they won't come in the evening, or at night.

MURIELLE

Nice meeting you, anyway, Mr. Simard.

LEO

I almost made a face at her. I wanted to get furious with my son, but I didn't have the strength, 'cause truth is, it got me all worked up inside to see my boy with a girl.

They climbed on that old motorcycle I drove for years with Eva's two arms hugging my heart. I wish you both the stamina to build happiness.

I watch them wrap themselves in mist.

And I go off to dream.

SEVENTEENTH WAVE

At the water's edge.

NIKI

The voice we hear over there is the voice of my body. I got beat up again. I shouldn't have gone near the old red dock. I thought Djoukie might be there because Goddess told me she took off in that direction.

DJOUKIE

Niki Simard! What are you doing in the high tide waters?

NIKI

I got a beating from some drug guys, I've lost a lot of blood. Don't be afraid of me.

DJOUKIE

I'm not afraid.

NIKI

Here, I bought you a sandwich ... Ooops! It's pretty squished.

> *DJOUKIE takes the sandwich and lets out two yelps, NIKI yelps back. They look at each other for a long time.*

DJOUKIE

Wow! Those guys really got you this time.

NIKI

They'll try again, but they can't kill me because I've already been visited by death.

Ever since I almost got myself deceased by a rock from the sky, I run with my head high, the wind at my heels, I know I can't die.

In the late spring, I was walking along the shore as the tide went out, with seven of our dogs. The sun was about to set, I was walking with my head tipped back so I could watch the clouds change colour, and then I saw a fiery tail sail by and crash on the little island to the north, 'bout an hour from here by canoe.

I froze. I saw it bounce back in the air. And there it was heading for me at top speed, I could hear it, I was sure I was going to die right then and there. Death was bearing down on me so fast. Then, I heard a loud whistling and plop! A dull thud at my feet. I had blood all over my legs, and my hands: one of my dogs had just died, smashed by the meteorite.

You can still see the red of his blood and his petrified flesh in the little craters. The smell of his burnt fur clung to me for weeks. The meteorite had become a tiny planet. No wonder, after a thousand-year race. I surrounded the remains of the dog with stones from low tide.

Here, take it.

DJOUKIE

I don't want your old rock.

You, the one I'm taking by the arm, answer me: You think you know death, but a life, ha! What's it like, a life? How do people see their lives in their heads? How do you feel about life, what do you understand about life? C'mon, answer me, where is the hidden meaning of life?

I began drinking coffee when I was eleven, yesterday I stopped. I love chips, but I decided to stop eating them. Once I smoked a whole pack of cigarettes in two hours, to see if I liked smoking. I threw up for an hour. I try to follow diets I can't stay on. I masturbate, but I also practice abstinence. Do this, stop doing that. Is that what life's about? Is that what Joelle means by giving life its due? If I talk too much, I get dizzy; if I shut my trap, I swell up with pain, so, I bark.

DJOUKIE barks. She barks again ... NIKI joins in.

NIKI
We've found each other at last. Come, my love, we'll be together for eternity. French me with love.

DJOUKIE
French a sickie. Your breath stinks. I hate guys who get beaten up; after they get punched silly, they play victim so everybody pities them.

NIKI
Love to the rescue! Love to the rescue!

DJOUKIE
Let go of me! I can't breathe, I can't breathe! I'm suffocating, suffocating, suffocating.

NIKI
Djoukie! Love to the rescue! Love to the rescue!

And the midnight blue fog swallowed her up as she fled.

EIGHTEENTH WAVE

In the mobile home, GODDESS is whispering in JOELLE's ear.

GODDESS

I speak these words to you, sister of my heart: I can still smell my grandmother's smokehouse and the fish hanging to dry.

I can still smell winter, in the days when the women braided rawhide with their strong hands all puffy from working in the damp. I can still smell, so vivid, the wood soaked in boiling water to bend the body of the snowshoe, and the strips of softened hide, and the steam that remained deep in our bones for hours.

We often followed the families who went hunting or fishing. We'd bring back moose, pheasants, hares and trout. We tanned the hides of the mink, the muskrats and beavers.

I can still smell the pine trees, the birch, the forest floor, the campfire in the tent. I don't know if you can still remember, Joelle.

JOELLE whispers in GODDESS's ear.

JOELLE

Yes, Goddess. I remember the smiles on our faces when we trekked through the woods all the way to the river to reach our hunting grounds. We had to paddle to Duck Lake. We portaged when the river wasn't canoeable because of the rapids.

My trout, my first trout, do you remember, you helped me bring it ashore. We were barely seven years old. My mother had to help us pull it out of the water. What a monster, it was such a big trout.

I miss our land, Goddess.

NINETEENTH WAVE

At the top of the cliff.

CHARLES

On this island, anything can happen. Just five minutes ago, you could've cut the fog with a knife and now, the wind is blowing harder and harder.

MURIELLE

Nobody can see us here, especially in the dark.

CHARLES

Why take so many paths just to screw?

MURIELLE

I didn't bring you to the top of the cliff to screw, I want you to do me a favour.

CHARLES

No, don't get me involved in some deal ...

MURIELLE

You see the tourists going home on the ferry. When I see them visiting our island, I wonder if they're just pictures because they just pass by and we'll never see them again. Ghosts in the flesh. I'm afraid that's what they think about me, that I don't exist, that I'm not really real. Nobody takes anybody into account. I don't want to be a passing ghost in the eyes of others.

When I'm gone, people will give me an identity. They'll say: The deceased Murielle Latraverse, the one who threw herself off the cliff in order to exist ... but I need you, in order to do it. I won't have the courage otherwise. Push me into the void so I can exist at last.

CHARLES

Kill you! Are you crazy?!

MURIELLE

You could do it, you're a criminal.

CHARLES

If you say that once more, I just might kill you.

MURIELLE

Do it, in memory of our ... Don't leave!

She shouts to the bottom of the cliff.

Help, help, do a gynecological test on me, I was raped last night. I still have the sperm of Mr. Charles Simard in my vagina!

CHARLES

With the wind tonight, nobody can hear you.

MURIELLE

Say what to who, anyway. I leave my words here, on the ground.

She backs away from the edge of the cliff to take a running start.

One, two ... at go, I'm going to do it. One, two, three, go.

I run, the moon shines down on me, I can see the surprise on Charles's face, he shouts: Don't do that, you're too beautiful.

Pardon?!

CHARLES
Don't do that, you're too beautiful.

MURIELLE
Really! You like how I look?

CHARLES
Yes, you're a pretty girl, I like you a lot.

MURIELLE
It's corny to cry when a guy finds you pretty but, when
it's the first time anyone's ever said it—

CHARLES
I care about you a lot.

MURIELLE
Ah! That's too much, I melt!

TWENTIETH WAVE

*COYOTE appears, carrying a lantern in one hand and
a pail full of small fry in the other. He notices GODDESS
in the dark.*

COYOTE
Goddess!? What are you doing here on the jetty?

GODDESS
I was looking for you, Coyote. You back from your
moonlight fishing?

COYOTE
If you're going to stand there looking haunted, you
better go home.

GODDESS

    … because of my tears.

    Take me in your arms.

COYOTE

    They're already full.

GODDESS

    I just remembered that I dreamed about the two of us last night.

    I was holding you by the leg: Let's live inside each other, come live on my land, I was asking you.

COYOTE

    What did I answer?

GODDESS

    Your soil is too spongy.

COYOTE

    I'm going to cook up a pan of small fry, you coming?

GODDESS

    In my dream, I was calling out to you, thrashing around in front of you, so my flesh would become a mountain with rocky ridges: Coyote! And you came to live in Goddess's den.

COYOTE

    Look, I stink of fish, I'm soaking wet, I still haven't eaten and in a little while, I'm sure we'll be all over each other, and then you'll be even more rumpled. So, don't take us for figures from the Garden of Eden.

    Get a move on, Goddess!

      He exits.

GODDESS

Don't take my dream lightly ... Coyote, I can't see a
thing!

COYOTE

Follow the scent of your animal.

TWENTY-FIRST WAVE

Outside the Gaz-O-Tee-Pee.

JOELLE

Last night, behind the garage, I tried to stay awake
around the fire, in case my daughter came back.

I fell asleep as soon as the wind stopped howling.

> *SIMON appears. He takes a last sip of his second bottle
> of red liquor. REX barks. JOELLE speaks, her eyes closed,
> like a sleepwalker.*

I know I'm dozing under my closed eyes, yet I can see
him coming towards me, Simon, the soldier, holding a
bottle.

Stop smiling at me.

Even if my mouth remains shut, like my eyes, I can
hear myself shout at him: Go away. I've failed at sex,
I've failed at love, I've failed at family life. My heart is
empty. There was a time when I was furious at men.
I've slept with guys who really wanted to fall in love, I
hooked them for six months. Once they were well
harpooned, I'd leave, with their best friend or their
brother or their father. I made a fool of so many guys,
I finally felt so heartsick I thought I'd choke. Don't
enter my life, I've got no heart.

SIMON

I'm holding your hand, and I speak these words: So, why do you come to me in my dreams at night? Why do you call me to lie on your body?

In every dream, I see myself preparing us for love, and suddenly, all of me becomes a sex that enters you, deep into your belly, and there I discover a little Joelle who's crying. Why are you calling me? To console you?

REX barks. JOELLE awakes with a start.

JOELLE

Djoukie? Who's there? Rex, calm down! Ah, Simon!

What are you doing here at this hour?

SIMON

Watch this, I'm hot.

I take off my shirt, I'm already barefoot.

JOELLE

Leave me alone, I'm not in the mood.

SIMON

Life flows from every pore of my body.

SIMON begins a strange dance.

JOELLE

Stop your go-go-boy nonsense, or I'll sic my dog on you.

SIMON

The flames of your fire can't burn my skin. I'm dancing both feet in the embers. Touch me, touch me, tonight, I am full of life.

JOELLE

Go away, you're scaring me.

REX barks again.

SIMON

I'm all yours, if you want me.

JOELLE

Don't come near me or I'll stab you with my knife.
Back off!

SIMON

Simon wants Joelle.

JOELLE

There, you bastard!

SIMON

Hit me again.

JOELLE

There, there!

SIMON

Again! I'm full of life, full of life.

JOELLE

I want to kill you, erase you from my sight.

SIMON

Joelle, let's mend our hearts.

He shouts, dancing, then falls. REX stops barking.

JOELLE

I drag him to my room, lie him on my bed. I don't
know what happened. I hit him with all my might. Not
a trace of blood, not a single wound.

Beat.

SIMON

Yesterday, I saw you in my kitchen, I was speaking
these words to you: While I peel the potatoes, take me

by surprise, act a bit dirty, I won't resist, run your hands through my hair, grab me by the hips, turn me around, push my ass against the counter, don't say a thing, lift up your skirt, press your sex against mine, put your tongue in my mouth, I'll still be holding a half-peeled potato in one hand, the peeler in the other, make love to me on the kitchen floor.

Afterwards, while we ate love-mashed potatoes, we said sweet words to each other, so life could reclaim a place in our heads.

Two bodies united, that should be enough to remake life.

JOELLE
And now ... euhh ... I'm gone.

TWENTY-SECOND WAVE

In the Simards' yard.

LEO
Often, in the middle of the night, the forty-two bitches who sleep in my room stand up on all fours and wait while I go piss. When I walk by my boys' room, I look at them. My Niki, even sound asleep, has a smile stamped on his face, and my oldest always has a face carved in pain. I love them.

After, I lie back down in my squeaky bed, I look at the forty-two balls of fur on the floor who'll fall back to sleep with me.

CHARLES enters.

The sun has risen and here's Mr. Charles coming
home to bed!

CHARLES

Pa-Leo, on my way here, I passed the SDA truck.

LEO

Don't move, I'll get my gun.

LEO exits. NIKI enters.

NIKI

(*carrying a bag of groceries*) Hi, brother. Guess what,
that's right, I'm in love with her.

CHARLES

Tell me, was it a beating that bruised you like that?
Answer me.

NIKI

Don't worry about it, my brother I love. I can't see
where I'm going, I'm blinded by love.

CHARLES

We've got to take care of you, you're a scary sight!

LEO returns with his rifle.

LEO

Hold on, our wounded lover! This morning, you're
not going anywhere, we've got a battle ahead!

NIKI

Pa-Leo, let me hug you, and you too, my brother.
Don't be mad because I took some groceries and …
I'm running away.

LEO

Niki!

TWENTY-THIRD WAVE

Outside the Gaz-O-Tee-Pee.

GODDESS
    Joelle, there's a customer.

    Oops, sorry! A man in Madam Joelle's bed! Stay there,
    I'll take care of it. By the way, Simon: the gas is for the
    SDA truck.

    SIMON hurries off. NIKI enters.

NIKI
    Goddess, is Djoukie here?

GODDESS
    No, my pup. Try to find her for us.

JOELLE
    Tell her I really want to talk to her.

    NIKI exits. COYOTE appears.

COYOTE
    Hey, Joelle! Simon just took off?

    *He picks up the empty bottle of red liquor. COYOTE starts
    to laugh extravagantly.*

    Oh! One of the two bottles I gave Simon. There's not
    a drop left.

    He smells the neck of the bottle.

    It must've packed quite a punch. It was strong stuff, I
    doubled the recipe.

    How was it? You're not answering me?

    JOELLE punches him in the face.

TWENTY-FOURTH WAVE

In the Simards' yard.

SIMON

Mr. Simard, there are two vets who'd like to examine your dogs.

LEO

You and your two white gorillas should take your hounding somewhere else. The islanders are unforgivable. I take in all the bastard pups they abandon and this is how I'm treated! When you think I'm the one who cures their dogs from the misery of straying.

SIMON

Your dogs are sick, Mr. Simard.

LEO

They accept their suffering to embrace the beauty of their soul, lad. Their bodies might be sick, but you can see their inner vitality in their eyes.

He fires a shot into the air.

You can't take them away from me. These dogs are the victims of time, they're in touch with the invisible.

CHARLES

Pa-Leo, Simon's trying to help us.

LEO

(*to SIMON*) Stay where you are.

SIMON

You have a good heart, but maybe the kennel's too big for you.

Gunshot.

Charles, tomorrow we'll have to come back with the police.

Gunshot.

LEO

Charles, back up, he'll infect you.

CHARLES

(*to SIMON*) I'll try to reason with him.

TWENTY-FIFTH WAVE

As daylight turns to twilight.

NIKI

As the moon rises over the path that leads to the sea wall on Rocky Point, I see my love, at last.

Don't be scared, Djoukie!

DJOUKIE

(*startled*) Idiot!

NIKI

Sorry. Still on the run? Where are you going?

DJOUKIE

To Rocky Point, to escape the mental cases who are chasing me.

NIKI

I'm following you, because I'm ahead of myself in love.

DJOUKIE

Tough luck for you, we'll never catch up with each other because I'm behind in love.

NIKI

Sometimes there can be collisions of love, an
awakening.

DJOUKIE

Go away.

NIKI

I think going to these rages on the shore is dumb, I
think it's stupid to go bullrushing in a girl's pond.
Everybody does that, it's ordinary, like death.

DJOUKIE

Go away. I can bite off your tongue. I'm the daughter
of a dog.

*DJOUKIE barks, NIKI starts to bark and howl. They bark
at each other.*

NIKI

You hear that, the dogs are answering us. I'm the son
of a bitch, too.

DJOUKIE

Stupid! People call you a son of a bitch because in the
school newspaper you denounced the names of the
parents who beat the dogs you rescue.

NIKI

No, you don't understand. I never saw my mother. She
died when I was born. Pa-Leo had a bitch nurse me,
that's why I'm the son of a bitch.

NIKI starts barking again.

Careful, there's no path over there, Djoukie!

The fog stifled Djoukie's scream, as she tumbled into
the darkness of her anger.

Djoukie, my love! My love!

TWENTY-SIXTH WAVE

LEO is phoning JOELLE.

LEO

This is Leo calling Joelle.

JOELLE

It's late, Leo Simard.

LEO

Since we're tied to each other by the fact that your daughter is leading my Niki astray, you shouldn't act so shocked. That's not how I brought up my son.

JOELLE

Leo, don't start bragging, I've got my own troubles.

LEO

My dogs can't stay still, as if they sensed some calamity. So, I'm talking to you over the wire like this to say that Coyote, when he came to deliver my bags of bones, he told me that your daughter and my son are down by the old sea wall at Rocky Point. I can't leave my kennel for one minute tonight, so I'm asking you to go fetch that girl of yours, then my Niki will come home.

TWENTY-SEVENTH WAVE

By the old sea wall at Rocky Point, DJOUKIE is moaning with pain.

NIKI

Djoukie, you could've broken your neck and died. Are you dizzy? Don't be scared, I just want to place my lips of love on yours.

He kisses her tenderly.

DJOUKIE
Mmmm. That's nice. Again.

They kiss again.

DJOUKIE
Again!

They kiss again.

NIKI
Again?!

They kiss again.

DJOUKIE
Let's sleep in our clothes under the stars.

TWENTY-EIGHTH WAVE

In his yard, COYOTE is preparing the recipe for his aphrodisiac punch. He is speaking-chanting.

COYOTE
I hear the call of sex
ringing in my testicles!
My whole belly is buzzing.
I think of tits
And my legs swell with blood
and run, run
my heart stops beating
my big dick and my brain
are one howling ball of drool.
I can taste, I can taste, I can taste
the salt of a woman's sea
in my mouth.

The throb of sex, that's me! Ha, ha, ha!
The throb of sex, that's me! Ha, ha, ha!

> *COYOTE starts laughing extravagantly. He looks at his mauve drink.*

Oops! Maybe I put a bit too much. Too bad! Who cares, who cares, who cares, we'll see what happens, because tomorrow night, there'll be another rage!

And I sneak off.

TWENTY-NINTH WAVE

On the shore, at night.

CHARLES

Who's there? Murielle? I'd given up on you, it's so late.

MURIELLE

I had a fight with my parents. Oh! Your ephemeral sculptures are amazing. I love them! I can't believe how frivolous I am.

CHARLES

Don't say that, you lighten my thoughts, Murielle. I'm so heavy, so dark inside.

MURIELLE

My parents said, if I go out with you, I'll become a criminal and a whore to boot ... and that one day you'll kill me. If I insist upon loving you, they're going to kick me out.

It makes me so sad to say it, but I have to leave you. I can't stand hurting them.

CHARLES

And you don't care about hurting me?

MURIELLE

I'm running, running away from you.

CHARLES

And I'm running after you.

MURIELLE

No, Charles!
Yes, Charles!
Take me away with you!

THIRTIETH WAVE

By the old sea wall at Rocky Point.

JOELLE

Djoukie! I know you're hiding here. You won't come
see me so I'll shout it to you through the dark of
night. You want to know who your father is? Your
father is some strangers!

When we were 15, Goddess and I ran away. On the
road, some guys picked us up, got us drunk and
dragged us into the woods. They beat us and raped us.

We went back home. Two months later we were both
pregnant and we decided that life would become life.
Our fathers and our brothers didn't want us to keep
the babies from two white-tailed strangers.

GODDESS

Joelle, where are you, sweetie?

JOELLE

Over here, Goddess!

GODDESS appears.

Come help me. Djoukie, Goddess will tell you, too.

GODDESS

It's true, Djoukie. The men forced us to leave the Reserve.

JOELLE

That's how we lost all our rights. Even if we wanted to go back to our land, Djoukie, our people would make us feel unwelcome.

GODDESS

That's how we ended up with a little exile cheque so we could start a new life as white women. Two months later, we'd drunk it all in a bar, barred from our old life.

JOELLE

Goddess had a miscarriage. She told me: We'll be two mothers for your baby.

GODDESS

Djoukie, we swore to each other we'd never breathe a word of this to you.

Come home, sweetheart!

JOELLE

Djoukie, answer us!

Silently, DJOUKIE has crept closer in the dark.

DJOUKIE

I'm listening to you, Ma.

JOELLE

My little girl, my little girl, the earth is painful, too painful.

GODDESS
Sweetheart, my little girl, too.

JOELLE
Djoukie! One desperate night, after Goddess's
husband died, when you were barely four years old—

GODDESS
I remember, we went outside one spring night, with
no clothes on.

JOELLE
I was running, you were running around the gas
pumps, we were shouting:

GODDESS
Look at my body.

GODDESS AND JOELLE
Look how ugly I am.

GODDESS
Ugly enough to freeze the sky.

JOELLE
Ugly enough to melt the earth.

GODDESS AND JOELLE
Look at this body that has no home, I'd like to break
it.

GODDESS
Hurt it.

JOELLE
Demolish it.

GODDESS
Assassinate it.

JOELLE
Why, Ma? Why did you let them kick us off our native land?

GODDESS and JOELLE stomp and rage.

GODDESS
It's burning!

JOELLE
It's burning!

GODDESS AND JOELLE
It's burning, burning!

DJOUKIE comes to join them.

DJOUKIE
Ma! Goddess!

She stomps with GODDESS and JOELLE, they join hands in a circle and howl long and loud.

THIRTY-FIRST WAVE

Loud howling which slowly fades. The voices of the characters are united in suspended time.

DJOUKIE
In the morning, the red, gold and orange sun will tickle our faces.

COYOTE
Yes, but it's still twilight.

NIKI
It won't be long. Look, the sun is rising.

MURIELLE

Off the calm surface of the water, the morning sun raises wisps of mist that will become today's clouds.

DJOUKIE

Where will we be today?

CHARLES

The wind carries wafts of low tide, it smells good.

SIMON

The sun rolls in on waves of blue.

GODDESS

'Round noon, the earth moves closer to the sun.

LEO

Its brightness even sneaks into the pockets of shadow.

NIKI

What will we do at noon?

DJOUKIE

We have reached the hour when the light almost blinds us.

JOELLE

Before the sun begins its slow, heavy descent.

LEO

In the morning, the earth swells with heat, in the afternoon, the heat fills our houses.

GODDESS

The sun created the wind, a scheme to make evening come swallow the colours.

NIKI

What will have become of us this evening?

COYOTE

And so, day brings daytime all day long, and night in turn brings nighttime to destroy what day created, and humans are trapped at the heart of this eternal quarrel.

The sounds of the rage party on the shore can be heard.

The end of suspended time.

THIRTY-SECOND WAVE

Outside the Gaz-O-Tee-Pee, DJOUKIE and NIKI are lying on the ground.

COYOTE

The light on the horizon barely illuminates our faces appalled by what happened during the rage.

GODDESS

That boy lying there, breathless, on the wooden table, is Niki, the lover.

The girl lying there, like a fallen tree, lifeless, sapless, is my sweetheart, Djoukie, the half-breed. The woman I take in my arms, my heart's sister, is inconsolable.

JOELLE

What happened? After our reunion, Djoukie asked my permission to spend the night on the sea wall with her friend, Niki. She promised she'd be home for supper the next day.

LEO

Niki, I'm holding your head to tell you I wish you could've stopped being lost in the haze of blue skies. Mother of Mars! Dying like this!

COYOTE

Goddess, I swear, I didn't organize that kind of rage.

CHARLES

Why, Niki, why didn't you ever tell me they beat you up because of me?

JOELLE

What happened? And where were you, Goddess?

GODDESS

I spent the day with Coyote, preparing his party. Something important had happened between us, Joelle.

I'd whispered in his ear real words of love.

COYOTE

For real?

GODDESS

Yes, like crazy.

COYOTE

Now you can come live with me.

GODDESS

I've told you hundreds of times what my heart feels for you.

COYOTE

Always drunk! It's the first time you've told me sober and the first time it was announced in a dream.

GODDESS

Try to understand, Joelle, I was so happy we'd decided to spend the rage at the lookout at Buzzards Bay, to celebrate our new life.

COYOTE

I thought Charles could replace me as D.J. in the jeep.

CHARLES

I was driving by his place on my motorcycle: just give me time to move Murielle into our house.

MURIELLE

Because yesterday morning, my parents kicked me out.

LEO

If I let you live here with my son, first, you have to stop calling me old limp balls. Second, the two of you are going to search for my son Niki and bring him back home. You better be more reliable than Joelle.

MURIELLE

You can count on us, Mr. Simard.

LEO

No bowing and scraping, fashion plate, go put your two bags of clothes in Charles's room. By the time you come home, I'll have cooked a nice supper … for my daughter-in-law.

I waited in vain, no one came home. Mother of Mars!

SIMON

Everything is so fragile. In the afternoon, I stopped by to see you: Joelle, I've got a lead for a contractor. He'll make you a good price. If you want, we can share the cost. It would make me really happy.

I feel like telling you: use me, use me.

JOELLE

Don't ask me to love you, I don't know how.

Maybe you could, nothing else, just take me in your arms, very, very slowly?

SIMON

Everything is so fragile.

JOELLE

Joelle is calling Djoukie.

LEO

Leo is calling Niki!

GODDESS

The voices we hear are the voices of Djoukie and Niki.

DJOUKIE

Djoukie is calling her ... friend.

NIKI

Do you want to go home now?

DJOUKIE

No, not at all, do you?

NIKI

No, I could spend my whole life with you. I just said that
because we've been here all day, sitting on the sea wall at
Rocky Point, without saying a word to each other.

DJOUKIE

Are you bored?

NIKI

With my heavenly rock, I'm going to write to you ...
here, on this stone.

DJOUKIE

What does that mean, I, L, U?

NIKI

There, do you want my meteorite?

DJOUKIE

(*taking the meteorite*) Give me a hint.

NIKI

    ILYouuu.

DJOUKIE

    ILYouuu! Wha ... ? Oh!

NIKI

    What did you understand?

DJOUKIE

    L, O ... you know the rest.

NIKI

    Go ahead, say it!

DJOUKIE

    L, O, V, E.

NIKI

    Say the word.

DJOUKIE

    No, I'm not the type.

NIKI

    Write it!

DJOUKIE

    Djoukie, heart, Niki.

NIKI

    I love you, I love you, I love you. She just wrote: I love you, for me.

    Niki is calling love!

DJOUKIE

    Djoukie is calling love!

NIKI

    Love is calling love.

LEO

In the late afternoon, I got drunk on one beer.

My sons, my sons! You're leaving me to rot on my own.
I opened the kennel and frightened my dogs out with
gunshots! They ran off like scared rabbits. There's
only one left. Now the SDA is gonna look dumb!

JOELLE

In the late afternoon, I killed my dog Rex.

I told Simon: Together, we'll raise your puppy, give
him a good home. I also said to him: Come, make life
with me, come make life with me, sweetly.

Suspended time.

LEO

Eva! I drape myself in stardust. Ah! I fly up into the
sky, all the way to the creamy white moon. It's so small,
I can sit on it.

I feel like I'm in our bedroom and the moon is
suspended in the corner of a ceiling made of burlap
… Wait, it doesn't work! When I lower my head, I can
see the blue earth. I'm really suspended in space and
the burlap screen prevents me from seeing the rest of
the universe. I want to know what's on the other side.
Do you know, Eva?

I take a little metal cylinder I made for myself. I always
keep it on me. I pierce a hole in the burlap and I look
through the end of my cylinder, a sidereal wind blows
on the pupil of my eye. On the other side, I can see, in
a magnificent silence, two planets circling 'round each
other, as if they were caught in an eternal embrace. Is
that us, Eva? Eva!

End of suspended time.

JOELLE

Goddess, tell me how she ended up on that damned shore.

COYOTE

Niki and Djoukie landed there, from the water, with Leo's old dinghy.

GODDESS

Goddess is calling Djoukie!

DJOUKIE

Niki, the tide is rising, let's drift into shore.

NIKI

Look, the waves are taking us to the remains of one of my brother's sculptures.

The guys who are always after me are there on the shore.

DJOUKIE

Stop! I'll beat you with this oar, if you take another step.

NIKI

The guys wade into the water up to their knees, tear the oar away from Djoukie and she falls into the water. They pull on the moorings and tip me out of the boat. They pelt me with rocks from Charles's sculpture, my head is bleeding.

DJOUKIE

I scramble out of the water: Stop, you're going to kill him! Let him go, you bunch of hopeless mental cases.

Even though his head is wagging from side to side, he's still wearing his big smile. And that drives them crazy.

NIKI

They beat me harder and harder.

DJOUKIE

With the meteorite in my hand, I jump on the back of one of the guys. He throws me onto the ground and knocks me out.

NIKI

My love! I called for help three times before I passed out.

COYOTE

I had just arrived on the shore with Charles to set up our gear. Usually, I would have heard him, I've got a good ear.

CHARLES

Pa-Leo, you know, we could have saved them, but the dogs from the kennel, that you'd just let loose, were howling and running around like crazy.

GODDESS

By dark, I was at the top of the cliff with Coyote. We were having a picnic, just the two of us, out in the open, in the warm, moist wind.

From where we were, we could see everything.

Coyote, look down there on the shore, the rage is beginning.

DJOUKIE

I can feel a dog's tongue licking my cheek. I wake up.

Niki! Niki!

NIKI

Kiss me.

DJOUKIE
> Yes, I'm kissing you.

NIKI
> Don't let go.

> I'm dying.

DJOUKIE
> Niki!

> I can see the glow of a fire. I pick up my planet of love. I carry you on my back.

GODDESS
> From the belvedere, I could see the flames of the fire flattened by the wind. I recognized Djoukie approaching with someone on her back and a dog leading the procession. Djoukie was screaming:

DJOUKIE
> Help!

> Niki, don't leave me alone in this junkpile of loveless mental cases.

NIKI
> Djoukie, I'm dying from too many blows on the head.

DJOUKIE
> To the rescue! Somebody! Rescue my love!

CHARLES
> Charles is calling Niki.

LEO
> What am I going to do without you, Niki, your smile lit up my life! Eva!

JOELLE
> Joelle is calling Djoukie!

COYOTE

The ragers wouldn't stop chanting:
We want starry skies, we want sweet sex.
And all those dogs barking on the island.

> *In the distance, like a haunting refrain, voices can be heard chanting:*

VOICES

We want starry skies, we want sweet sex.

MURIELLE

Charles, come quick! Your brother's head is bleeding.

CHARLES

Niki!

Because of the sand, I was running in slow motion like when you're being chased by a beast in a dream.

SIMON

In war or in ritual, when men let off steam, they're always the same.

GODDESS

The island capsized.

DJOUKIE

Love to the rescue! Love to the rescue!

LEO

Answer her, someone!

GODDESS

Coyote went tearing down the path from the belvedere.

Then I saw the scene from hell, Joelle. I thought the ragers were picking up rocks to stone the dog that was running ahead of Djoukie.

I was wrong, they were aiming at Djoukie. Joelle, it was Djoukie, our sweetheart, they were stoning to death.

COYOTE
Me and Charles arrived too late.

GODDESS
I screamed so loud the wind sent my voice whirling 'round the island.

JOELLE
Joelle is calling her daughter.

DJOUKIE
I'm dying, Ma.

Can you hear my voice in the sky, it's calling to you and to all humanity:

Love to the rescue!

> *After a moment of silence, DJOUKIE and NIKI begin to bark. The two DOGS from the beginning move downstage and look into the audience. The barking is contagious, the other characters imitate the young couple. They all stomp and bark louder and louder, for a long time. Blackout.*
>
> *Then, all nine characters begin to spin 'round and 'round. The two dogs, still downstage, on either side of the stage, facing each other, turn their heads away from the audience, toward the stage. The actors exit.*
>
> *The two DOGS watch the audience leave the theatre.*

The End.